IT'S TIME TO EAT THAI ICED TEA

It's Time to Eat THAI ICED TEA

Walter the Educator

SKB

Silent King Books
A WhichHead Entertainment Imprint

Disclaimer

This book is a literary work; the story is not about specific persons, locations, situations, and/or circumstances unless mentioned in a historical context. Any resemblance to real persons, locations, situations, and/or circumstances is coincidental. This book is for entertainment and informational purposes only. The author and publisher offer this information without warranties expressed or implied. No matter the grounds, neither the author nor the publisher will be accountable for any losses, injuries, or other damages caused by the reader's use of this book. The use of this book acknowledges an understanding and acceptance of this disclaimer.

It's Time to Eat THAI ICED TEA is a collectible early learning book by Walter the Educator suitable for all ages belonging to Walter the Educator's Time to Eat Book Series. Collect more books at WaltertheEducator.com

USE THE EXTRA SPACE TO TAKE NOTES AND DOCUMENT YOUR MEMORIES

THAI ICED TEA

It's time for a drink so cold and sweet,

It's Time to Eat

Thai
Iced
Tea

Thai iced tea is a special treat!

Orange and creamy, cool and bright,

Sipping this tea feels just right.

In a tall glass, it's layered and bold,

Tea on the bottom, ice cubes cold.

A swirl of cream floats on top,

One sip, and we just can't stop!

The tea is rich, with hints of spice,

Sweet and smooth, oh, so nice!

With every sip, a taste so neat,

Thai iced tea is fun to greet.

Orange and frosty, creamy and light,

A colorful drink, such a pretty sight.

We swirl the straw, mix it around,

And watch the colors twist and bound.

It's Time to Eat

Thai
Iced
Tea

A hint of vanilla, a touch of sweet,

This tea is magic, such a treat!

We drink it slow, or take big sips,

It cools us down from head to lips.

For sunny days or times to share,

Thai iced tea is beyond compare.

It's cool and tasty, silky and fun,

A drink that's loved by everyone!

With ice that clinks and tea that glows,

Every sip makes our happiness grow.

A frosty drink on a sunny day,

Thai iced tea takes us away.

The orange hue, the creamy mix,

Feels like magic, like little tricks.

It's Time to Eat

Thai
Iced
Tea

A drink so sweet, a drink so cool,

Thai iced tea is our golden rule.

So gather around, take a big sip,

Let that creamy tea touch your lip.

With friends and family, it's a blast

Thai iced tea is a treat that lasts!

From the first sip to the very last drop,

This icy drink makes us hop!

A sweet and creamy, frosty cheer

It's Time to Eat

Thai
Iced
Tea

Thai iced tea, we hold so dear!

ABOUT THE CREATOR

Walter the Educator is one of the pseudonyms for Walter Anderson. Formally educated in Chemistry, Business, and Education, he is an educator, an author, a diverse entrepreneur, and he is the son of a disabled war veteran. "Walter the Educator" shares his time between educating and creating. He holds interests and owns several creative projects that entertain, enlighten, enhance, and educate, hoping to inspire and motivate you. Follow, find new works, and stay up to date with Walter the Educator™

at WaltertheEducator.com

9 798330 552290